VIOLIN   2ND EDITION

THE BEST OF
The Beatles

T0084129

ISBN 978-1-4234-1047-8

HAL•LEONARD® CORPORATION

7777 W. BLUEMOUND RD. P.O. BOX 13819 MILWAUKEE, WI 53213

Visit Hal Leonard Online at
www.halleonard.com

CONTENTS

ALL MY LOVING

VIOLIN

Words and Music by JOHN LENNON
and PAUL McCARTNEY

ACROSS THE UNIVERSE

VIOLIN

Words and Music by JOHN LENNON
and PAUL McCARTNEY

Slowly and smoothly

ALL YOU NEED IS LOVE

VIOLIN

Words and Music by JOHN LENNON
and PAUL McCARTNEY

AND I LOVE HER

VIOLIN

Words and Music by JOHN LENNON
and PAUL McCARTNEY

BACK IN THE U.S.S.R.

VIOLIN

Words and Music by JOHN LENNON
and PAUL McCARTNEY

THE BALLAD OF JOHN AND YOKO

VIOLIN

Words and Music by JOHN LENNON
and PAUL McCARTNEY

BECAUSE

VIOLIN

Words and Music by JOHN LENNON
and PAUL McCARTNEY

Moderately slow

BIRTHDAY

VIOLIN

Words and Music by JOHN LENNON
and PAUL McCARTNEY

Moderately fast Rock

BLACKBIRD

VIOLIN

Words and Music by JOHN LENNON
and PAUL McCARTNEY

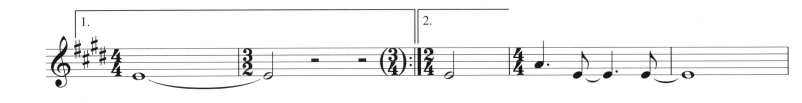

CAN'T BUY ME LOVE

VIOLIN

Words and Music by JOHN LENNON
and PAUL McCARTNEY

COME TOGETHER

VIOLIN

Words and Music by JOHN LENNON
and PAUL McCARTNEY

A DAY IN THE LIFE

VIOLIN

Words and Music by JOHN LENNON
and PAUL McCARTNEY

DAY TRIPPER

VIOLIN

Words and Music by JOHN LENNON
and PAUL McCARTNEY

DEAR PRUDENCE

Violin

Words and Music by JOHN LENNON
and PAUL McCARTNEY

DO YOU WANT TO KNOW A SECRET?

VIOLIN

Words and Music by JOHN LENNON
and PAUL McCARTNEY

DRIVE MY CAR

VIOLIN

Words and Music by JOHN LENNON
and PAUL McCARTNEY

Moderately, with a beat

EIGHT DAYS A WEEK

VIOLIN

Words and Music by JOHN LENNON
and PAUL McCARTNEY

ELEANOR RIGBY

VIOLIN

Words and Music by JOHN LENNON
and PAUL McCARTNEY

EVERY LITTLE THING

VIOLIN

Words and Music by JOHN LENNON
and PAUL McCARTNEY

THE FOOL ON THE HILL

VIOLIN

Words and Music by JOHN LENNON
and PAUL McCARTNEY

FROM ME TO YOU

VIOLIN

Words and Music by JOHN LENNON
and PAUL McCARTNEY

GET BACK

VIOLIN

Words and Music by JOHN LENNON
and PAUL McCARTNEY

GIRL

VIOLIN

Words and Music by JOHN LENNON
and PAUL McCARTNEY

GOLDEN SLUMBERS

VIOLIN

Words and Music by JOHN LENNON
and PAUL McCARTNEY

GOOD DAY SUNSHINE

VIOLIN

Words and Music by JOHN LENNON
and PAUL McCARTNEY

GOT TO GET YOU INTO MY LIFE

Violin

Words and Music by JOHN LENNON
and PAUL McCARTNEY

A HARD DAY'S NIGHT

VIOLIN

Words and Music by JOHN LENNON
and PAUL McCARTNEY

HELLO, GOODBYE

VIOLIN

Words and Music by JOHN LENNON
and PAUL McCARTNEY

HELP!

VIOLIN

Words and Music by JOHN LENNON
and PAUL McCARTNEY

HELTER SKELTER

VIOLIN

Words and Music by JOHN LENNON
and PAUL McCARTNEY

HERE COMES THE SUN

VIOLIN

Words and Music by
GEORGE HARRISON

HERE, THERE AND EVERYWHERE

VIOLIN

Words and Music by JOHN LENNON
and PAUL McCARTNEY

HEY JUDE

VIOLIN

Words and Music by JOHN LENNON
and PAUL McCARTNEY

I FEEL FINE

Violin

Words and Music by JOHN LENNON
and PAUL McCARTNEY

Bright Rock

I AM THE WALRUS

VIOLIN

Words and Music by JOHN LENNON
and PAUL McCARTNEY

Slowly

I SAW HER STANDING THERE

VIOLIN

Words and Music by JOHN LENNON
and PAUL McCARTNEY

Moderately bright, with a beat

I SHOULD HAVE KNOWN BETTER

VIOLIN

Words and Music by JOHN LENNON
and PAUL McCARTNEY

I WANT TO HOLD YOUR HAND

VIOLIN

Words and Music by JOHN LENNON
and PAUL McCARTNEY

I WILL

VIOLIN

Words and Music by JOHN LENNON
and PAUL McCARTNEY

I'LL CRY INSTEAD

VIOLIN

Words and Music by JOHN LENNON
and PAUL McCARTNEY

I'LL FOLLOW THE SUN

Violin

Words and Music by JOHN LENNON
and PAUL McCARTNEY

I'M A LOSER

VIOLIN

Words and Music by JOHN LENNON
and PAUL McCARTNEY

Moderately

I'M HAPPY JUST TO DANCE WITH YOU

VIOLIN

Words and Music by JOHN LENNON
and PAUL McCARTNEY

I'VE JUST SEEN A FACE

VIOLIN

Words and Music by JOHN LENNON
and PAUL McCARTNEY

IF I FELL

VIOLIN

Words and Music by JOHN LENNON
and PAUL McCARTNEY

IN MY LIFE

VIOLIN

Words and Music by JOHN LENNON
and PAUL McCARTNEY

IT WON'T BE LONG

VIOLIN

Words and Music by JOHN LENNON
and PAUL McCARTNEY

IT'S ONLY LOVE

VIOLIN

Words and Music by JOHN LENNON
and PAUL McCARTNEY

Moderately

JULIA

VIOLIN

Words and Music by JOHN LENNON
and PAUL McCARTNEY

LADY MADONNA

VIOLIN

Words and Music by JOHN LENNON
and PAUL McCARTNEY

LET IT BE

VIOLIN

Words and Music by JOHN LENNON
and PAUL McCARTNEY

THE LONG AND WINDING ROAD

VIOLIN

Words and Music by JOHN LENNON
and PAUL McCARTNEY

LOVE ME DO

VIOLIN

Words and Music by JOHN LENNON
and PAUL McCARTNEY

LUCY IN THE SKY WITH DIAMONDS

VIOLIN

Words and Music by JOHN LENNON
and PAUL McCARTNEY

MAGICAL MYSTERY TOUR

VIOLIN

Words and Music by JOHN LENNON
and PAUL McCARTNEY

MARTHA MY DEAR

VIOLIN

Words and Music by JOHN LENNON
and PAUL McCARTNEY

MICHELLE

VIOLIN

Words and Music by JOHN LENNON
and PAUL McCARTNEY

NO REPLY

VIOLIN

Words and Music by JOHN LENNON
and PAUL McCARTNEY

NORWEGIAN WOOD
(This Bird Has Flown)

VIOLIN

Words and Music by JOHN LENNON
and PAUL McCARTNEY

NOWHERE MAN

VIOLIN

Words and Music by JOHN LENNON
and PAUL McCARTNEY

Moderately bright

OB-LA-DI, OB-LA-DA

VIOLIN

Words and Music by JOHN LENNON
and PAUL McCARTNEY

OCTOPUS'S GARDEN

VIOLIN

Words and Music by RICHARD STARKEY,
JOHN LENNON and PAUL McCARTNEY

PAPERBACK WRITER

VIOLIN

Words and Music by JOHN LENNON
and PAUL McCARTNEY

PENNY LANE

VIOLIN

Words and Music by JOHN LENNON
and PAUL McCARTNEY

PLEASE PLEASE ME

VIOLIN

Words and Music by JOHN LENNON
and PAUL McCARTNEY

P.S. I LOVE YOU

VIOLIN

Words and Music by JOHN LENNON
and PAUL McCARTNEY

REVOLUTION

VIOLIN

Words and Music by JOHN LENNON
and PAUL McCARTNEY

Moderate Rock and Roll Shuffle

RUN FOR YOUR LIFE

VIOLIN

Words and Music by JOHN LENNON
and PAUL McCARTNEY

Moderately

SGT. PEPPER'S LONELY HEARTS CLUB BAND

VIOLIN

Words and Music by JOHN LENNON
and PAUL McCARTNEY

SHE LOVES YOU

VIOLIN

Words and Music by JOHN LENNON
and PAUL McCARTNEY

SHE'S A WOMAN

VIOLIN

Words and Music by JOHN LENNON
and PAUL McCARTNEY

SOMETHING

Violin

Words and Music by
GEORGE HARRISON

STRAWBERRY FIELDS FOREVER

VIOLIN

Words and Music by JOHN LENNON
and PAUL McCARTNEY

TELL ME WHY

VIOLIN

Words and Music by JOHN LENNON
and PAUL McCARTNEY

THANK YOU GIRL

Words and Music by JOHN LENNON
and PAUL McCARTNEY

THINGS WE SAID TODAY

VIOLIN

Words and Music by JOHN LENNON
and PAUL McCARTNEY

THIS BOY
(Ringo's Theme)

VIOLIN

Words and Music by JOHN LENNON
and PAUL McCARTNEY

TICKET TO RIDE

VIOLIN

Words and Music by JOHN LENNON
and PAUL McCARTNEY

TWIST AND SHOUT

VIOLIN

Words and Music by BERT RUSSELL
and PHIL MEDLEY

Moderately, with a beat

WE CAN WORK IT OUT

VIOLIN

Words and Music by JOHN LENNON
and PAUL McCARTNEY

WHEN I'M SIXTY-FOUR

Violin

Words and Music by JOHN LENNON
and PAUL McCARTNEY

WHILE MY GUITAR GENTLY WEEPS

VIOLIN

Words and Music by
GEORGE HARRISON

WITH A LITTLE HELP FROM MY FRIENDS

VIOLIN

Words and Music by JOHN LENNON and PAUL McCARTNEY

THE WORD

VIOLIN

Words and Music by JOHN LENNON
and PAUL McCARTNEY

YELLOW SUBMARINE

VIOLIN

Words and Music by JOHN LENNON
and PAUL McCARTNEY

YES IT IS

VIOLIN

Words and Music by JOHN LENNON
and PAUL McCARTNEY

YESTERDAY

Violin

Words and Music by JOHN LENNON
and PAUL McCARTNEY

YOU CAN'T DO THAT

VIOLIN

Words and Music by JOHN LENNON
and PAUL McCARTNEY

YOU WON'T SEE ME

VIOLIN

Words and Music by JOHN LENNON
and PAUL McCARTNEY

Moderately

YOU'RE GOING TO LOSE THAT GIRL

VIOLIN

Words and Music by JOHN LENNON
and PAUL McCARTNEY

YOU'VE GOT TO HIDE YOUR LOVE AWAY

Violin

Words and Music by JOHN LENNON
and PAUL McCARTNEY

Moderately

YOUR MOTHER SHOULD KNOW

VIOLIN

Words and Music by JOHN LENNON
and PAUL McCARTNEY